cooking the RUSSIAN way

Chicken kiev, a gourmet dish named after the capital of the Ukraine, is often served with scalloped potatoes. (Recipes on pages 32 and 33.)

cooking the
RUSSIAN way

GREGORY & RITA PLOTKIN

PHOTOGRAPHS BY ROBERT L. & DIANE WOLFE

easy menu
ethnic
cookbooks

Lerner Publications Company ■ Minneapolis

Editor: Vicki Revsbech
Drawings by Jeanette Swofford
Map by Larry Kaushansky and Jeanette Swofford

Photographs on pages 8, 10, and 12 courtesy of H. J. Lerner

The page border for this book is based on the onion-shaped
domes that are typical of prerevolutionary Russian architecture.

Special thanks to my mother, Sima Plotkin,
who spent 30 years teaching people how to cook
and took an active part in putting this book together – G.P.

Library of Congress Cataloging-in-Publication Data

Plotkin, Gregory.
    Cooking the Russian way.

    (Easy menu ethnic cookbooks)
    Includes index.
    Summary: Introduces the cooking and food habits
of the Soviet Union, including such recipes as borsch,
chicken kiev, and beef stroganoff, and provides brief
information on the geography and history of the country.
    1. Cookery, Russian—Juvenile literature. 2. Soviet
Union—Social life and customs—Juvenile literature.
[1. Cookery, Russian. 2. Soviet Union—Social life and
customs] I. Plotkin, Rita. II. Wolfe, Robert L. ill.
III. Wolfe, Diane, ill. IV. Title. V. Series.
TX723.3.P58   1986   641′.0947   86-7155
ISBN 0-8225-0915-6 (lib. bdg.)

Manufactured in the United States of America

5 6 – I/JR – 99 98 97 96 95 94

**Sirniki are rich cheese pancakes that make a tasty
breakfast or supper. (Recipe on page 39.)**

CONTENTS

Dairy Cows

Cod

Herring

Arctic Ocean

Potatoes

LITHUANIA   LATVIA   ESTONIA

BYELORUSSIA

Leningrad

Lvov

MOLDAVIA

Fruit

Kiev

UKRAINE

Moscow

Gorki

Ural Mountains

Lena River

RUSSIA (RSFSR)

Salmon

Ob River

Yenisey River

Vegetables

Volga River

Novosibirsk

Black Sea

Sheep

GEORGIA

Caucasus Mountains

ARMENIA

Lemons

AZERBAIJAN

Caspian Sea

Sturgeon

Sugar Beets

Corn

Grain

Aral Sea

Cotton

Tashkent

Yablonovyy Mountains

Altai Mountains

KAZAKHSTAN

TURKMENISTAN

KIRGHIZIA

UZBEKISTAN

TAJIKISTAN

Flag of the USSR

■ European Plain
□ Ural Mountains
□ Aral-Caspian Lowland
■ West Siberian Plain
■ Central Siberian Plateau
■ East Siberian Uplands

INTRODUCTION

Russia is a name that is familiar all over the world. It is what many people call the country whose official name is the Union of Soviet Socialist Republics (USSR). Russia is actually the name of the USSR's largest republic. The USSR, or Soviet Union, is a union of people of different ethnic backgrounds, which makes it a land of great variety. The people living in one part of the country are very different from those who live in other regions. They may speak another language, have their own unique customs, and even vary in physical appearance. The cuisine of the USSR is as varied and interesting as its people, but from *borsch* to caviar, it is all delicious.

THE LAND

The USSR stretches across eastern Europe and northern and central Asia. It is larger than all but three of the continents, and nearly every kind of land and climate is included in its boundaries. There are places in the Soviet Union above the Arctic Circle that do not see the sun for six months of the year, and there are regions that never have snow.

The *European Plain* in the west is the most well-developed and populous area in the USSR. It contains most of the country's major cities, including Moscow, Leningrad, and Kiev, and is home to most of the USSR's industries. As its name suggests, the European Plain is relatively flat, except for the Caucasus Mountains in the south. The *Aral-Caspian Lowland* in the south is mostly desert and grassy lowlands. Separating the European USSR from the Asian USSR is the *Ural Mountains* region, which runs from the Arctic Circle to the Aral Sea. Siberia is a sparsely populated area east of the Ural Mountains that experiences extremely cold temperatures. It is divided into three regions. The *West Siberian Plain*, a swampy, forested region, is more than a million miles square and is the largest level area in the world. The forests continue into the *Central Siberian Plateau*, where there are many mountains and canyons. The *East Siberian Uplands* is a rugged wilderness that is the USSR's most mountainous region.

THE HISTORY

The Soviet Union is a young country, less than 100 years old, but the history of its largest republic—Russia—dates back over one thousand years. The Slavs established the Russian state in 800 A.D. In 1547, Ivan IV (also known as Ivan the Terrible) became the first of a series of powerful leaders, called czars, who would rule Russia for almost 400 years. The czars gradually purchased and conquered territory until, by the reign of Peter the Great in the late 1600s, Russia had grown to be a powerful nation about the size of today's Soviet republic of Russia.

The 1800s were a time of political unrest in Russia that foreshadowed the revolution that was to come in the following century.

Leningrad's *Spas na Krovi* (Church of the Resurrection), with its onion-shaped domes, is reflected in the waters of the Griboyedov Canal.

The workers and the middle class were unhappy with the terrible working conditions and extreme inequalities in the Russian system. In January 1905, workers made a peaceful march on Czar Nicholas II's Winter Palace to ask for reform. The czar's troops fired on the crowd, killing more than 100 people, and violence broke out all over Russia as people protested what came to be known as "Bloody Sunday." The czar was forced to allow some reforms, including the establishing of an elected Duma, or parliament, but it wasn't enough.

In 1917, Nicholas II was deposed, and the Bolshevik party, led by Lenin, seized power in the October Revolution. The Bolsheviks changed their name to the Communist Party of the Soviet Union and, in 1922, established the Union of Soviet Socialist Republics. The boundaries of Russia and, subsequently, the USSR were constantly changing until World War II when the nation established its last four republics for a total of fifteen. Today, the Soviet Union is still controlled by the Communist Party, and it has become one of the most powerful nations in the world.

THE FOOD

More than two-thirds of the Soviet people live in the Slavic republics of Russia, Byelorussia, and the Ukraine, which makes Slavic cuisine the most popular food in the USSR. Food is very important to the Slavs, and they like it to be rich, filling, and, most of all, plentiful. Much of today's Slavic cuisine is based on the cooking of the peasants of prerevolutionary Russia. Bread, a staple food of the peasants, is still one of the most important foods in all three Slavic regions. The Ukraine is famous for its delicious breads and has been called "the breadbasket of Europe."

Borsch is another food that was handed down by the peasants. It is a hearty soup made from beets and any of a variety of other ingredients including cabbage, carrots, potatoes, onions, and meat. There are almost as many versions of this traditional soup as there are Slavic cooks.

Slavic cooking also has its roots in the food favored by the nobility of prerevolutionary Russia. The most striking characteristic of this cuisine was the amount served at one time.

After dinner, families in the Soviet Union enjoy dessert, coffee, and conversation.

An upper-class dinner would have course after course of rich, delicious food, beginning with a substantial *zakuska*, or appetizer, which usually featured the Russian delicacy caviar. The main meal often included meat, poultry, and fish, as well as soup, salad, vegetable, and a rich dessert. Although very few, if any, Slavs eat on such a large scale today, many of the dishes of the time, such as beef stroganoff and salad olivier, are still favorites.

The Baltic Republics—Latvia, Lithuania, and Estonia—are located on the coast of the Baltic Sea on the northwest border of the Soviet Union. Because of their northern climate, agriculture here is not as well developed as in other republics. This is, however, one of the few areas in Russia where dairy cows are raised. The cooking of the Baltic Republics, especially Estonia, is very similar to that of the Scandinavian countries. It is a simple, hearty cuisine with a strong emphasis on potatoes, bread, dairy products, pork, and a great variety of fish.

Between the Caucasus Mountains and the countries of Turkey and Iran, there is an area where the people live longer than anywhere else in the world. This area, called the Caucasus, includes the republics of Armenia, Georgia, and Azerbaijan. The cooking of the Caucasus has a definite Middle Eastern flavor. Lamb is common throughout the area and is often served in hearty stews or grilled on skewers to make the popular *shashlyk*. The Middle Eastern influence is especially strong in Armenia in such dishes as *dolmas*, grape leaves stuffed with rice and meat, and *baklava*, a rich honey-nut pastry. The Middle Eastern staples of chickpeas, pine nuts, and cracked wheat are an important part of Armenian cooking. The republic of Moldavia on the Romanian border, is often grouped with the Caucasian republics because of the similarities in their cuisines.

The republic of Kazakhstan and the four central Asian republics—Uzbekistan, Turkmenistan, Kirghizia, and Tajikistan—make up the southernmost part of the USSR. Although visitors find the cooking of these regions different than what they're used to, they find it tasty nonetheless. The trademark dish is *plov*, a mixture of rice, lamb, and spices that is similar to the pilafs served in the Middle

This Ukrainian woman has come to Chernovtsy to sell her turkey at the market.

East. A wealth of delicious fruit, including figs, grapes, peaches, apples, cherries, and over 1,000 different kinds of melon, is grown in Uzbekistan and is an important part of the cuisine. As in most of the USSR, bread is also important to this region, and most people bake their own from family recipes instead of buying it in a store.

The Soviet Union has such a huge variety of cuisines spread over so many millions of miles that it is difficult for a visitor to sample them all. A good cross section of Soviet cooking, however, is available in the many restaurants in the capital city of Moscow. A number of Moscow's restaurants are named after Soviet republics or their capitals and feature the food of that region. Visitors can dine on the cuisine of Uzbekistan at the Tashkent Restaurant, try Ukrainian cooking at the Ukraina or sample traditional Russian fare at the Moskva.

With the recipes in this book, you, too, can prepare a meal containing dishes from the various regions of the USSR. You're sure to love the delicious flavors of this vast and varied country.

BEFORE YOU BEGIN

Cooking any dish, plain or fancy, is easier and more fun if you are familiar with its ingredients. Russian cooking makes use of some ingredients that you may not know. You should also be familiar with the special terms that will be used in various recipes in this book. Therefore, *before* you start cooking any of the Russian dishes in this book, study the following "dictionary" of special terms very carefully. Then read through the recipe you want to try from beginning to end.

Now you are ready to shop for ingredients and to organize the cookware you will need. Once you have assembled everything, you can begin to cook. It is also important to read *The Careful Cook* on page 44 before you start.

COOKING UTENSILS

colander—A bowl with holes in the bottom and sides. It is used for draining liquid from a solid food.

Dutch oven—A heavy pot with a tight-fitting domed lid that is often used for cooking soups or stews

rolling pin—A cylindrical tool used for rolling out dough

slotted spoon—A spoon with small openings in the bowl. It is used to pick solid food out of a liquid.

spatula—A flat, thin utensil, usually metal, used to lift, toss, turn, or scoop up food

tongs—A utensil used to grasp food

whisk—A small wire utensil used for beating foods by hand

COOKING TERMS

beat—To stir rapidly in a circular motion

boil—To heat a liquid over high heat until bubbles form and rise rapidly to the surface

garnish—To decorate with a small piece of food such as parsley

A sharp knife is best for mincing food, but remember to be careful when using it.

grate—To cut into tiny pieces by rubbing the food against a grater

knead—To work dough by pressing it with the palms, pushing it outward, and then pressing it over on itself

mince—To chop food into very small pieces

preheat—To allow an oven to warm up to a certain temperature before putting food in it

sauté—To fry quickly over high heat in oil or fat, stirring or turning the food to prevent burning

simmer—To cook over low heat in liquid kept just below its boiling point. Bubbles may occasionally rise to the surface.

steep—To soak a substance, such as tea, in hot water to extract flavor

SPECIAL INGREDIENTS

bay leaf—The dried leaf of the bay (also called laurel) tree, used to season food

bread crumbs—Tiny pieces of stale bread made by crushing the bread with the bottom of a glass or a rolling pin. Packaged bread crumbs can be bought at grocery stores.

buttermilk—A milk product made from soured milk

cinnamon—A spice made from the bark of a tree in the laurel family, which is available ground and in sticks

corn syrup—A sweet syrup made from cornstarch

cornstarch—A fine white starch made from corn, commonly used for thickening sauces and gravies

dill—An herb whose seeds and leaves are both used in cooking. Dried dill is also called **dill weed.**

farmer cheese—A pressed white cheese made from whole or partially skimmed milk

feta cheese—A crumbly, white cheese made from goat's milk

nutmeg—A fragrant spice, either whole or ground, that is often used in desserts

olive oil—An oil made by pressing olives. It is used in cooking and for dressing salads.

ricotta cheese—A white cheese made with whole or skim milk that resembles cottage cheese

scallion—A variety of green onion

sunflower oil—A cooking oil made from sunflower seeds

yeast—An ingredient used in baking that causes dough to rise, which is available in either small, white cakes called compressed yeast or in granular form called active dry yeast

A RUSSIAN MENU

Below is a menu for a typical day of Russian cooking. The Russian names of the dishes are given, along with a guide on how to pronounce them.

ENGLISH	PO-RUSSKY	PRONUNCIATION GUIDE
MENU	MENOO	meh-NYOO
Breakfast	*Zavtrak*	ZAV-track
Pancakes with Sour Cream	Blini so Smetanoy	blee-NEE SO smeh-TAH-noy
Sunday Breakfast	*Voskresenye Zavtrak*	vohsk-reh-SEN-yeh ZAV-track
Boiled Potatoes in Vinegar and Oil	Kartoshka v Mundire v Uksuse e Masle	kar-TOSH-kah VEH moon-DEE-reh VEE OOK-soo-syeh EE MAS-lyeh
Sausage	Sardelka	sar-DEL-kah
Rye Bread	Rzhanoi Khleb	r'zhah-NOY HLEB
Indian Tea	Indisky Chai	een-DEE-skee CHAH-ee
Dinner	*Obed*	oh-BYED
I	I	
Appetizer	Zakuska	zah-KOOS-kah
Beet Soup	Borsch	BORSH
Chicken Kiev	Kotleta Po-kievsky	kot-LEH-tah POH KEE-ehv-skee
Scalloped Potatoes	Otvarnaya Kartoshka	ot-var-NAH-yah kar-TOSH-kah
Kompot	Kompot	kom-POHT

ENGLISH	PO-RUSSKY	PRONUNCIATION GUIDE
MENU	MENOO	meh-NYOO
Dinner	**Obed**	oh-BYED
II	II	
Vegetable Salad Vesna	Ovoshnoy Salat Vesna	oh-vish-NOY sah-LAHT VEZ-nah
Meat Bouillon	Myasnoy Bullyon	myahs-NOY bool-YON
Pirozhki	Pirozhki	pee-ROZH-kee
Beef Stroganoff	Beef Stroganov	BEEF STROH-gah-nahv
Noodles or Straw	Lapsha eli Kartoshka	lahp-SHAH EE-lee
Potatoes	Solomkoy	kar-TOSH-kah sol-AHM-koy
Raspberry *Kisel*	Malinoviy Kisel	mah-LIH-no-vee kee-SEL
Supper	**Uzhin**	OO-zhin
I	I	
Cheese Pancakes	Sirniki	SEER-nee-kee
Sour Cream	Smetana	smeh-TAH-nah
Milk	Moloko	moh-loh-KOH
II	II	
Appetizer	Zakuska	zah-KOOS-kah
Salad Olivier	Salat Olivye	sah-LAHT oh-lee-VYEH
Vinegret	Vinegret	vee-neh-GRET
Studen	Studen	STOO-den
Coffee	Kofe	KOH-fe
Honey Spice Cake	Kovrizhka Medovaya	kov-RISH-kah meh-DOH-vah-yah

BREAKFAST/
Zavtrak

According to a Russian saying, you should
"Eat breakfast yourself, share the dinner with
a friend, but give the supper to your enemy!"
This shows the importance of the first meal
of the day. During the week, breakfast is
usually eaten at about 8:00 A.M. It is a very
filling meal that gives people enough energy
for the first and most productive part of
the day.

Pancakes/
Blini

Blini *served with sour cream and milk*
or tea is a very typical Russian breakfast.

4 cups all-purpose flour
2 cups buttermilk
1 egg
½ teaspoon salt
1 tablespoon sugar
½ to 1 cup warm water (optional)
¼ cup sunflower oil for frying

1. Place flour in a large mixing bowl.
Gradually add buttermilk, beating well
with a spoon to prevent lumps from
forming.
2. Add egg, salt, and sugar and stir until
blended. Mixture should be the consis-
tency of pancake batter. If too thick,
stir in ½ cup warm water.
3. Set batter in a warm place for 10 to
15 minutes.
4. Lightly grease a small frying pan with
1 teaspoon oil. Heat pan for several

seconds over medium heat.

5. Pour ¼ cup batter into pan, quickly swirling pan so a thin, even layer covers the bottom. (If batter has thickened, beat in more warm water.) When edge of pancake lifts easily from pan, carefully flip over with a spatula.

6. When other side lifts easily from pan, remove pancake, place on a plate, and cover with a cloth towel. Repeat with remaining batter, adding more oil to the pan when necessary. Serve warm with sour cream, jam, and butter.

Serves 4 to 6

Often served with jam or sour cream, *blini* are also delicious with cottage cheese, mushrooms, herring, and even caviar.

A hearty breakfast of boiled potatoes, sausage with mustard, homemade rye bread, and hot tea with lemon is a good way to start the day.

SUNDAY BREAKFAST/
Voskresenye Zavtrak

Sunday breakfast is different than breakfasts during the week. On Sundays, breakfast is usually eaten between 9:00 and 10:00 A.M. It is a hearty meal that all members of the family look forward to as a time to be together.

Boiled Potatoes/
Kartoshka v Mundire

While some foods are difficult to find in parts of the Soviet Union and too expensive for the ordinary person to afford, potatoes are always available. Russians can eat potatoes three times a day. During World War II when food was scarce, this nutritious vegetable saved the lives of hundreds of thousands of people. Boiled potatoes are usually served with dill pickles and sauerkraut.

8 medium potatoes
1 teaspoon salt

1. Wash potatoes thoroughly, place in a large saucepan, and cover with water.
2. Bring water to a boil over high heat. Add salt, reduce heat to medium-low, and cover, leaving cover slightly ajar so steam can escape. Cook until potatoes can be easily pierced with a fork.
3. Drain potatoes in a colander and set aside until cool enough to handle. Peel and serve warm with vinegar and oil dressing.

Vinegar and Oil Dressing:

2 tablespoons vinegar
1/4 teaspoon salt
1/8 teaspoon pepper
1/3 cup sunflower oil

1. In a medium bowl, mix all ingredients except oil with a whisk.
2. Slowly add oil, beating constantly with whisk.

Serves 4 to 6

Rye Bread/
Rzhanoi Khleb

The USSR is known the world over for its rye bread. The secret to making good rye bread is to not add too much flour and to be patient enough to let the bread rise fully. This recipe makes a delicious, dense loaf that is well worth the time and the effort it takes to make it.

2 packages active dry yeast (4½ teaspoons)
1 cup warm water (105° to 115° F)
⅓ cup dark corn syrup
4½ to 5½ cups dark rye flour
2 teaspoons salt

1. In a large bowl, dissolve yeast in 1 cup warm water. Stir in corn syrup and set aside for 5 minutes until yeast mixture foams. If after 5 minutes yeast mixture has not started to foam, the water is too cold or too hot or the yeast is too old. Discard the yeast mixture and try again.
2. Add 2½ cups flour to the yeast mixture, a little at a time, and beat with a spoon until smooth. Stir in salt.
3. Set bowl in a warm place, cover with a cloth towel (not terry cloth), and let rise for 30 minutes.
4. Add 2 to 3 more cups flour, a half cup at a time, stirring after each addition. When dough becomes difficult to stir, turn out onto a floured surface and knead in flour with your hands until dough is stiff but still slightly sticky. Form dough into a ball.
5. Wash and dry bowl. Place dough in bowl, cover with a cloth towel, and set in a warm place. Let rise for 2½ to 3 hours or until dough almost doubles.
6. Turn dough out onto floured surface and, with floured hands, form into a loaf. Place loaf in a well-greased 9- by 5-inch baking pan, cover tightly with plastic wrap, and return to warm place to rise for 1 hour.
7. Preheat oven to 350°.
8. Bake for 30 to 35 minutes. (Bread will not brown much.)

Makes 1 loaf

Sausage/
Sardelka

Beef or pork sausage can be served for breakfast, dinner, or supper or as an appetizer. It is very popular because it makes an inexpensive and filling meal.

**1 1-pound smoked beef or pork
      sausage (such as kielbasa)**

1. Place sausage in a large pan and cover with water.
2. Bring water to a boil over medium-high heat. Boil for 5 to 7 minutes until meat is heated through. Serve hot with mustard.

Serves 4

Indian Tea/
Indisky Chai

Czar Peter the Great discovered Indian tea when he began trading with India in the 18th century. The rich aroma and delicious flavor of Indian tea have made this popular hot drink one of the Soviet Union's major imports from India.

**1 cup water per person
1 teaspoon tea leaves (or 1 teabag)
      for each 3 to 4 cups water**

1. In a teakettle or saucepan, bring water to a boil over high heat.
2. Rinse a teapot with hot tap water.
3. Place tea in teapot. Fill teapot ¾ full of boiling water and let steep for 5 to 7 minutes. Add remaining water.
4. If you used teabags, remove them from teapot. Serve hot with lemon and sugar.

In nearly every household in the USSR, some sort of *zakuska*, or appetizer, is eaten before the main meal.

DINNER/
Obed

Dinner, the main meal in the Soviet Union, is usually eaten between 12:00 and 2:00 P.M. It is a large meal consisting of three to four courses. Dinner starts with an appetizer; then a soup such as *borsch* or bouillon is served. This is followed by a main course of beef, pork, chicken, or fish and either potatoes, noodles, rice, or buckwheat. Fruit *kompot* usually concludes the meal.

Appetizer/
Zakuska

In Russia, the tradition of starting dinner with an appetizer may have begun in the countryside where people had to travel great distances to visit each other. Hosts would serve substantial zakuski *to their guests until everyone had arrived and dinner was served.*

½ **pound smoked herring**
½ **pound chopped liver**
6 **slices salami**
6 **slices ham**
6 **French rolls**
  dill pickles
  cherry tomatoes
  marinated mushrooms
  radishes
  various cheeses
  butter

Arrange ingredients on several large serving plates.

Serves 4 to 6

Beet Soup/
Borsch

Borsch is a hearty vegetable soup that is rich in vitamins. There are many ways to make borsch: *with beef, with chicken, or with no meat at all. It can contain any of a variety of vegetables.*

  4 **beef neck bones**
  2 **beets**
  2 **carrots**
  2 **onions, peeled**
12 **cups (3 quarts) water**
  3 **medium potatoes**
 ¼ **cabbage**
 ½ **green pepper**
  1 **bunch fresh parsley or 1 tablespoon dried parsley flakes**
 ¼ **teaspoon salt**
  2 **cups tomato juice**
  1 **teaspoon lemon juice pepper**
  6 **tablespoons sour cream**

1. Rinse neck bones with cold water and wash beets and carrots thoroughly. Cut 1 onion in half and place in a Dutch oven with neck bones, beets, and 1 carrot.

2. Add 11 cups water and bring to a boil over high heat. Reduce heat to medium and use a spoon to skim off foam that forms on the surface. Cook for 20 to 25 minutes or until vegetables are soft.

3. Remove vegetables from Dutch oven with tongs. Discard onion and set carrot and beets aside to cool. Remove neck bones and discard.

4. Peel potatoes and cut into quarters. Slice cabbage into strings and pepper into strips. Peel and slice raw carrot.

5. Add raw vegetables, parsley, salt, and 1 cup water and cook for 20 minutes.

6. Stir in tomato juice and cook for another 8 to 10 minutes.

7. Peel the cooked beets and carrot, grate or chop finely, and add to soup. Continue to cook for 10 to 15 minutes.

8. Add lemon juice before serving. If you used fresh parsley, remove from soup and discard. Serve in large bowls with pepper and 1 tablespoon sour cream.

Serves 6

Borsch (left) and meat bouillon *(right)* are two nutritious soups that include a variety of ingredients.

Meat Bouillon/
Myasnoy Bullyon

Meat bouillon is a rich, seasoned soup prepared with chicken, pork, beef, or lamb. Russians say that meat bouillon has curing powers and gives your body energy and strength.

1 2½- to 3-pound chicken
1 onion, peeled
1 carrot, peeled
1 bunch fresh dill or 1 tablespoon
**   dried dill weed**
1 bunch fresh parsley or 1 tablespoon
**   dried parsley flakes**
½ teaspoon salt

1. Wash chicken in cold water, place in a Dutch oven or large kettle, and cover with cold water.
2. Bring water to a boil over high heat. With a spoon, skim off foam that forms on surface of water.
3. After removing as much foam as possible, reduce heat to medium. Cut onion and carrot in half and add to soup. Cover and cook for 1 hour.
4. Add dill and parsley. (If you use fresh dill and parsley, wash thoroughly in cold water before adding to soup.)
5. Reduce heat to low, cover, and cook for 30 to 40 minutes or until chicken is tender. Add salt, stir, and cook for another 5 minutes.
6. With tongs, remove onion, fresh parsley, and fresh dill from kettle and discard.
7. Carefully remove chicken and remaining vegetables from soup and set on a plate to cool. When chicken is cool enough to handle, discard skin and remove meat from bones. Cut vegetables and meat into bite-size pieces and add to soup. Serve hot.

Serves 6

Pirozhki

This traditional Russian dish is suitable for any holiday table. Pirozhki *can be stuffed with meat, cabbage, rice, potatoes, or eggs.*

Filling:

4 tablespoons sunflower oil
3 medium onions, peeled
and chopped
1½ pounds ground beef
1 teaspoon salt
⅛ teaspoon pepper

1. In a large frying pan, heat 2 tablespoons oil over medium-high heat for 1 minute. Add onions and sauté until golden brown. Remove from pan and set aside.
2. Add remaining oil to pan and heat for 1 minute over medium-high heat. Add meat and cook until brown, mashing with a fork to break into small pieces. Drain off fat.
3. Place meat, onions, salt, and pepper in a blender. Cover and blend on maximum speed for 5 to 7 seconds. (If you don't have a blender, place meat in a large bowl and mash well with a fork.)

Dough:

2 cups all-purpose flour
⅛ teaspoon salt
1 egg
½ to ¾ cup water or skim milk
melted butter

1. In a medium bowl, mix flour, salt, and egg. Add liquid, a little at a time, until dough is stiff.
2. Knead dough for 2 to 4 minutes on a floured surface. (You will have to add more flour.) Roll out dough to ⅛-inch thickness with a rolling pin. With a glass or cookie cutter, cut out rounds of dough 3 inches in diameter.
3. Preheat oven to 400°.
4. Put 1 tablespoon filling on one half of each circle. Moisten edges of dough with a little water. Fold dough over filling and press edges together first with your fingers, then with the tines of a fork.
5. Place *pirozhki* on a greased cookie sheet and bake for 30 minutes or until golden brown. Brush with melted butter and serve at room temperature.

Makes 12 to 18 pirozhki

Pirozhki, straw potatoes, and vegetable salad can be eaten by themselves as a light supper or with other dishes for a more elaborate dinner.

Straw Potatoes/
Kartoshka Solomkoy

This dish is just one of dozens of ways to prepare potatoes Russian-style.

**4 large potatoes
   sunflower oil for frying
   salt**

1. Peel potatoes and cut into strips about 3 inches long and ¼ inch thick. Wash potatoes thoroughly and pat dry with paper towel.
2. Pour 1 inch of oil into a large frying pan. Heat oil to 370° over medium heat. (Use a fat thermometer to check temperature of oil.)
3. Carefully place potatoes in oil with a slotted spoon. Fry for 10 to 12 minutes, stirring gently to prevent sticking.
4. When potatoes are golden brown, carefully remove from oil with slotted spoon and drain on paper towel. Sprinkle with salt and serve hot.

Serves 4

Vegetable Salad Vesna/
Ovoshnoy Salat Vesna

Vegetable salad goes well with a variety of dressings. This recipe is made with sour cream, but it is also delicious when made with vinegar and oil or with mayonnaise.

**2 bunches radishes
1 bunch scallions
3 cucumbers, peeled
8 ounces feta cheese
1 tablespoon olive oil
1½ cups sour cream
½ teaspoon salt**

1. Wash vegetables well with cold water. Cut off roots and leaves of radishes and roots and ends of leaves of scallions.
2. Slice cucumbers and radishes into thin rounds. Cut cheese into ¼-inch cubes. Chop scallions finely.
3. In a large bowl, mix vegetables, cheese, oil, sour cream, and salt.

Serves 4 to 6

Scalloped Potatoes/
Otvarnaya Kartoshka

If Russia had to be identified with a fruit or vegetable, it would be the potato. The USSR grows more potatoes than any other country—about 30 percent of the world's potato crop.

2 to 2½ pounds new potatoes, peeled
1 medium onion, peeled
½ teaspoon salt
1 bunch dill or 1 tablespoon dill weed
¼ cup butter, melted
1 clove garlic, minced (optional)

1. Wash potatoes and onion and cut onion in half. Place potatoes and onion in large saucepan, cover with water, and add salt.
2. Bring water to a boil over high heat. Reduce heat to medium-low and cover, leaving cover slightly ajar so steam can escape. Cook potatoes about 20 minutes or until they can be easily pierced with a fork.
3. If using fresh dill, cut off and discard roots, wash thoroughly in cold water, and chop finely. Combine dill, melted butter, and garlic and set aside.
4. When potatoes are ready, drain well in a colander and discard onion. Return potatoes to pan. Pour butter mixture over potatoes, cover pan tightly, and shake well. Serve hot with chicken kiev.

Serves 4 to 6

Chicken Kiev/
Kotleta Po-kievsky

Although chicken kiev is a familiar dish in many parts of the world, few people realize that it originated in Russia. This gourmet dish is named after Kiev, the capital of the Soviet republic of the Ukraine.

4 boneless chicken breasts
¼ teaspoon salt
¼ teaspoon pepper
½ cup butter
1 clove garlic, crushed

**½ cup chopped fresh parsley or 3
    tablespoons dried parsley flakes
6 eggs
2 cups bread crumbs
    sunflower oil**

1. Place each piece of meat between 2 pieces of wax paper and beat with a hammer to flatten. Remove paper and sprinkle both sides of meat with salt and pepper.
2. In a small bowl, mash butter with a fork and stir in garlic and parsley. Divide into 4 equal portions.
3. Place a piece of meat on a flat surface. Place one portion of the butter mixture on the chicken breast's wider end. Fold each side over the butter and roll up the breast tightly (see diagram). Do the same with the other 3 breasts.
4. In a shallow dish, beat eggs well. Pour bread crumbs into another shallow dish. Dip a piece of chicken into eggs, coating thoroughly, then roll in bread crumbs until completely covered. Repeat 4 times with the same piece of meat and set aside.

Do the same with the other 3 breasts.
5. In a large frying pan, heat 1 inch oil over medium heat for 30 seconds. Carefully place chicken in pan with tongs and fry, turning frequently, until meat turns golden brown. Remove from pan with tongs and drain on paper towel.
6. Just before serving, pierce chicken kiev with a fork to let butter run out.

Serves 4

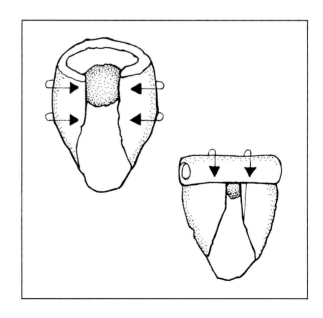

Beef stroganoff, which originated in Russia, is a popular dish served all over the world.

Beef Stroganoff/
Beef Stroganov

Beef stroganoff is known and loved in the United States and in many European countries. It originated in Russia in the 19th century when it was created for Count Stroganov.

3 tablespoons sunflower oil
4 medium onions, peeled
  and chopped
1½ pounds beef, sliced in short,
  thin strips
2 cups sour cream
1 pinch salt
1 pinch pepper
3 to 4 bay leaves

1. Heat oil in a Dutch oven over medium-high heat for 1 minute. Add onions and sauté, stirring frequently, until golden brown.
2. Add meat and stir well. Cover and cook for 5 minutes over medium heat. Remove cover and sauté meat and onions for another 5 minutes.
3. Stir in 1 cup hot water and cover. Continue cooking, adding 1 cup hot water every time water level gets low.
4. When meat is tender, add enough hot water to barely cover it and simmer 5 minutes.
5. Add sour cream, mix well, and simmer 5 minutes. Add salt, pepper, and bay leaves. Simmer for another 5 minutes.

Noodles:

6 ounces medium egg noodles
4 tablespoons butter
  dash of pepper
  fresh parsley for garnish

1. Cook noodles according to directions on package.
2. Drain in a colander and toss with butter and pepper.
3. Serve beef stroganoff hot over noodles. Garnish with parsley.

Serves 4 to 6

Kompot

Kompot is a drink that makes an excellent dessert or snack, and it can also be served instead of punch or soft drinks. It is made from fresh fruits in the summer and dried fruits in the winter. Kompot is most popular in the southern USSR, where many fruits are grown.

1 pound assorted fruits (or any one kind of fruit)
6 cups water
½ to 2 cups sugar
1 cinnamon stick
⅛ teaspoon nutmeg

1. Wash fruit in cold water and cut into small pieces (Cut apples and pears into quarters, plums in halves, and leave berries whole.) Remove pits and seeds.
2. Place fruit in a large kettle and add 6 cups water. Bring to a boil over high heat.
3. Reduce heat to low, add ½ cup sugar, and stir. Cover and simmer for 20 to 25 minutes.

4. Depending on the combination of fruits you have used, you may have to add more sugar. (Add sugar sparingly—if *kompot* tastes sweet when hot, it will taste even sweeter when cold.)
5. Add cinnamon and nutmeg and stir well. Simmer for another 10 minutes. *Kompot* can be served hot or cold.

Serves 6

Raspberry *Kisel/* Malinoviy Kisel

In the central and northern parts of the USSR, kisel is preferred to kompot. Kisel is an after-dinner drink that is served cold.

1 pound raspberries
½ cup cornstarch
8½ cups water
1 cup sugar
whipped cream for topping

1. Wash raspberries in cold water and place in large bowl. Crush well with the back of a spoon. Set aside.

2. In a small bowl, combine cornstarch with ½ cup water and stir until cornstarch is completely dissolved. Set aside.

3. In a large saucepan, combine sugar and 8 cups water and stir well. Bring to boil over high heat, stirring occasionally.

4. Add crushed fruit and cornstarch mixture to boiling syrup and stir until mixture begins to thicken.

5. Remove pan from heat and let *kisel* cool to room temperature before refrigerating. Serve chilled in glasses topped with whipped cream.

Serves 6

Desserts like honey spice cake, raspberry *kisel (front)*, and *kompot (back)* will satisfy everyone's sweet tooth. (Recipes on pages 36 and 43.)

Studen (front), **salad olivier** *(back left)*, **and** *vinegret (back right)* **taste best if refrigerated for five to eight hours before serving. (Recipes on pages 40, 41, and 42.)**

SUPPER/
Uzhin

In the USSR, supper is eaten between 6:00 and 8:00 P.M. It is usually the lightest meal of the day and sometimes consists of just one dish. However, if supper is eaten out at a restaurant or as a guest in someone's home, it becomes a combination of dinner and supper. This larger supper can include appetizers, soup, and sometimes dessert.

Cheese Pancakes/
Sirniki

Sirniki can be eaten for breakfast or supper and are served with sour cream, honey, or jam.

**2 pounds farmer cheese or
    ricotta cheese
1 egg
½ cup sugar, plus extra for sprinkling
½ teaspoon salt
1 to 1½ cups all-purpose flour**

sunflower oil for frying

1. In a large bowl, mash cheese with a fork. Add egg and mix well. Stir in sugar and salt.
2. Add flour, a little at a time, while kneading dough. Continue adding flour and kneading until dough can be shaped easily with hands.
3. Cover hands with flour and scoop up a piece of dough about the size of a medium apple. Roll dough into a ball between palms and press to form a pancake about 1 inch thick. Make 3 or 4 before frying.
4. Cover bottom of large frying pan with oil and heat over medium heat for 1 minute. Carefully place pancakes in pan with a spatula and fry for 3 to 4 minutes or until bottom is golden brown. Turn over and fry until second side turns golden brown.
5. Continue making and frying *sirniki*, adding more oil to pan when necessary, until dough is used up.
6. Sprinkle *sirniki* with sugar before serving.

Serves 6

Salad Olivier/
Salat Olivye

This gourmet dish may have come to Russia from France before the Russian Revolution of 1917. It is a festive addition to a holiday meal.

2 whole chicken breasts
1 medium onion, peeled
6 large potatoes
6 eggs
8 medium dill pickles
2 tablespoons olive oil
1 17-ounce can sweet peas, drained
2 cups mayonnaise, plus extra for garnish
¼ teaspoon salt
¼ teaspoon pepper
parsley, scallions, dill, or cooked egg yolks for garnish

1. Wash chicken in cold water and cut onion in half. Place chicken and onion in large saucepan, cover with water, and bring to a boil over high heat.

2. Cover pan, reduce heat to low, and simmer for 30 to 40 minutes or until chicken is tender. Remove from heat and let chicken cool to room temperature in broth. Discard onion.

3. While chicken is cooking, wash potatoes well, place in a large saucepan, and cover with water. Bring to a boil over high heat. Reduce heat to medium-low and cover pan, leaving cover slightly ajar so steam can escape. Cook until potatoes can be easily pierced with a fork. Drain in a colander and rinse with cold water until cool.

4. Place eggs in a large saucepan, cover with water, and bring to a boil over high heat. Remove from heat, cover pan, and let stand for 20 to 25 minutes. Rinse with cold water until cool.

5. Cool salad ingredients to room temperature before preparing salad. Discard chicken skin, remove chicken from bones, and cut into bite-size pieces. Peel potatoes and eggs. Cut potatoes, eggs, and pickles lengthwise into quarters, then chop into ¼-inch wedges. Place in a large bowl.

6. Add olive oil to salad and mix well.

Stir in sweet peas. Add mayonnaise, salt, and pepper and mix again.

7. To serve, place in a crystal or glass bowl, flatten the surface, and spread with a thin layer of mayonnaise. Garnish with chopped parsley, scallions, dill, or cooked egg yolk.

Serves 6 to 8

Vinegret

Vinegret is an old Russian recipe that is inexpensive to make and very nutritious. It is a common dish at school campuses.

6 medium potatoes
3 medium beets
3 medium carrots, peeled
6 dill pickles
1 medium onion, peeled
½ cup sauerkraut (optional)
⅓ cup olive oil
2 tablespoons vinegar
¼ teaspoon salt
¼ teaspoon pepper
   chopped parsley or dill for garnish

1. Wash potatoes, beets, and carrots well in cold water and place in 3 separate pans. Cover each with water and bring to a boil over high heat. Reduce heat to medium-low and cover, leaving cover slightly ajar so steam can escape. Cook for 20 to 25 minutes or until vegetables can be easily pierced with a fork.

2. Drain vegetables in a colander and rinse with cold water until cool. (Salad ingredients must be no warmer than room temperature when salad is prepared.)

3. Cut pickles and carrots lengthwise into quarters, then chop into ¼-inch wedges. Peel potatoes and beets and cut into ¼-inch cubes. Cut onion into half rings. Combine vegetables in large bowl, add sauerkraut, and mix well.

4. In a small bowl, combine oil, vinegar, salt, and pepper. Beat with a whisk for 2 minutes. Pour dressing over vegetables and mix well. Garnish with chopped parsley or dill.

Serves 6 to 8

Studen

Although the recipe for studen *originated in the Soviet republic of Russia, it is enjoyed in other parts of the country as well. Studen can also be made with beef or pork instead of chicken.*

2 tablespoons sunflower oil
3 large onions, peeled and finely
**   chopped**
3 large carrots, peeled and grated
1 2½- to 3-pound chicken, cut
**   into 8 pieces**
1 tablespoon minced garlic
**   pepper**
¼ teaspoon salt
3 bay leaves

1. In a Dutch oven, heat oil over medium heat for 1 minute. Add onions and sauté, stirring frequently, until golden brown.
2. Add carrots and continue to sauté for 10 minutes.
3. Wash chicken in cold water, rub with 1 teaspoon minced garlic, and sprinkle with pepper. Add to Dutch oven and cover. Cook for 7 to 10 minutes, stirring occasionally.
4. Add 1 cup hot water, stir, and replace cover. Simmer for 40 minutes, adding 1 cup hot water each time broth gets low.
5. Add salt, bay leaves, and remaining garlic. Simmer for 10 minutes.
6. Remove pan from heat. Remove chicken from pan with tongs and set aside. When cool enough to handle, remove meat from bones and cut into bite-size pieces.
7. When broth is cool, add chicken and stir. Pour *studen* into a 9- by 9-inch pan and refrigerate until fat solidifies on top. Carefully remove fat with a knife or spatula. Refrigerate overnight before serving.
8. Cut *studen* into square pieces and serve with horseradish or vinegar.

Serves 6

Honey Spice Cake/
Kovrizhka Medovaya

Honey spice cake used to be served during religious holiday celebrations in Russia. Today it is a common dessert that is especially popular with children.

2 eggs
½ cup brown sugar
2 cups all-purpose flour
½ teaspoon baking soda
1 cup honey
½ cup raisins
½ cup sliced almonds (or other nuts)

1. Grease and flour a 9- by 5-inch loaf pan. Preheat oven to 350°.
2. Beat eggs thoroughly in a small bowl. Add sugar and stir well.
3. Pour flour into a large mixing bowl. Add egg mixture and baking soda and stir well.
4. Add honey and mix for 10 minutes. Stir in raisins.
5. Pour dough into pan, level it out, and sprinkle with nuts.
6. Bake for 50 to 60 minutes or until toothpick stuck in the middle of cake comes out clean.
7. Serve with whipped cream or jam.

Makes 9 to 12 pieces

THE CAREFUL COOK

Whenever you cook, there are certain safety rules you must always keep in mind. Even experienced cooks follow these rules when they are in the kitchen.

1. Always wash your hands before handling food.
2. Thoroughly wash all raw vegetables and fruits to remove dirt, chemicals, and insecticides.
3. Use a cutting board when cutting up vegetables and fruits. Don't cut them up in your hand! And be sure to cut in a direction *away* from you and your fingers.
4. Long hair or loose clothing can easily catch fire if brought near the burners of a stove. If you have long hair, tie it back before you start cooking.
5. Turn all pot handles toward the back of the stove so that you will not catch your sleeve or jewelry on them. This is especially important when younger brothers and sisters are around. They could easily knock off a pot and get burned.

6. Always use a pot holder to steady hot pots or to take pans out of the oven. Don't use a wet cloth on a hot pan because the steam it produces could burn you.
7. Lift the lid of a steaming pot with the opening away from you so that you will not get burned.
8. If you get burned, hold the burn under cold running water. Do not put grease or butter on it. Cold water helps to take the heat out, but grease or butter will only keep it in.
9. If grease or cooking oil catches fire, throw baking soda or salt at the bottom of the flame to put it out. (Water will *not* put out a grease fire.) Call for help and try to turn all the stove burners to "off."

METRIC CONVERSION CHART

WHEN YOU KNOW		MULTIPLY BY	TO FIND	
MASS (weight)				
ounces	(oz)	28.0	grams	(g)
pounds	(lb)	0.45	kilograms	(kg)
VOLUME				
teaspoons	(tsp)	5.0	milliliters	(ml)
tablespoons	((Tbsp)	15.0	milliliters	
fluid ounces	(oz)	30.0	milliliters	
cup	(c)	0.24	liters	(l)
pint	(pt)	0.47	liters	
quart	(qt)	0.95	liters	
gallon	(gal)	3.8	liters	
TEMPERATURE				
Fahrenheit	(°F)	5/9 (after	Celsius	(°C)
temperature		subtracting 32)	temperature	

COMMON MEASURES AND THEIR EQUIVALENTS

3 teaspoons = 1 tablespoon

8 tablespoons = ½ cup

2 cups = 1 pint

2 pints = 1 quart

4 quarts = 1 gallon

16 ounces = 1 pound

INDEX

(recipes indicated by **bold face** *type)*

ABOUT THE AUTHORS

Gregory and Rita Plotkin were born in the Soviet Union, where they both learned to love cooking the Russian way. Gregory was a child actor and starred in four motion pictures before moving to the United States in 1972. He now works in television and film production in California. Rita is a student in Toronto, Canada, where she lives with their son, Robert.